W9-AZI-188

Essential Lives

MARK ZUCKERBERG

MARK ZUCKERBERG

FACEBOOK CREATOR

by Marcia Amidon Lusted

Montana Miller, PhD
assistant professor, Department of Popular Culture
Bowling Green State University

ABDO
Publishing Company

CREDITS

Published by ABDO Publishing Company, 8000 West 78th Street, Edina, Minnesota 55439. Copyright © 2012 by Abdo Consulting Group, Inc. International copyrights reserved in all countries. No part of this book may be reproduced in any form without written permission from the publisher. The Essential Library™ is a trademark and logo of ABDO Publishing Company.

Printed in the United States of America,
North Mankato, Minnesota
022011
032011

 THIS BOOK CONTAINS AT LEAST 10% RECYCLED MATERIALS.

Editor: Mari Kesselring
Copy Editor: Rebecca Rowell
Interior Design and Production: Marie Tupy
Cover Design: Kazuko Collins

Library of Congress Cataloging-in-Publication Data
Lusted, Marcia Amidon.
  Mark Zuckerberg : facebook creator / by Marcia Amidon Lusted.
     p. cm. -- (Essential lives)
  Includes bibliographical references and index.
  ISBN 978-1-61783-008-2
  1. Zuckerberg, Mark, 1984- 2. Facebook (Firm)--Juvenile literature. 3. Facebook (Electronic resource)--Juvenile literature. 4. Webmasters--United States--Biography--Juvenile literature. 5. Computer software developers--United States--Biography--Juvenile literature. 6. Businesspeople--United States--Biography--Juvenile literature. 7. Online social networks--Juvenile literature. I. Title.
  HM479.Z83L87 2012
  006.7'54092--dc22
  [B]
                                                    2011005614

TABLE OF CONTENTS

Chapter 1   Person of the Year   6

Chapter 2   Birth of a Computer Genius   16

Chapter 3   Harvard   26

Chapter 4   The Birth of Facebook   34

Chapter 5   Into the Real World   44

Chapter 6   The Harvard Connection Lawsuit   56

Chapter 7   Fact and Fiction   66

Chapter 8   Running Facebook   76

Chapter 9   Looking to the Future   86

Timeline   96

Essential Facts   100

Glossary   102

Additional Resources   104

Source Notes   106

Index   110

About the Author   112

Mark Zuckerberg is the creator of Facebook.

PERSON OF THE YEAR

On December 15, 2010, *Time* magazine chose its annual Person of the Year. *Time* claims that being named Person of the Year is "a recognition of the power of individuals to shape our world."[1] In this case, they chose someone who has not only shaped the world but who has actually changed the way people communicate. The choice was Mark Zuckerberg, the founder and creator of Facebook, a social networking site that almost 600 million people use every day on the Internet.

Time explained why Zuckerberg was chosen for this honor:

> *For connecting more than half a billion people and mapping the social relations among them (something that has never been done before); for creating a new system of exchanging information that has become both indispensable and sometimes a little scary; and finally, for changing how we all live our lives in ways that are innovative and even optimistic, Mark Elliot Zuckerberg is Time's 2010 Person of the Year.*[2]

But *Time*'s announcement was just the latest moment of media attention for Zuckerberg. At only 26 years old, he was named one of

Facebook's Popularity

Facebook has become the most popular social networking site on the Internet. As Facebook notes on its statistics page, "A January 2009 Compete.com study ranked Facebook as the most used social network service by worldwide monthly active users, followed by MySpace. *Entertainment Weekly* put it on its end-of-the-decade 'best-of' list, saying, 'How on earth did we stalk our exes, remember our co-workers' birthdays, bug our friends, and play a rousing game of Scrabulous before Facebook?' Quantcast estimates Facebook has 135.1 million monthly unique U.S. visitors in October 2010. According to Social Media Today as of August 2010, it is estimated that 41.6 percent of the U.S. population has a Facebook account."[3]

the youngest billionaires in the United States on the *Forbes* magazine list of wealthy people in 2010. Also in 2010, the story of Zuckerberg's student days at Harvard University and the creation of Facebook became a major motion picture called *The Social Network*. Some of Zuckerberg's decisions about Facebook have come under fire from users who are concerned about privacy and marketing issues. Yet, Facebook continues to grow in popularity every day. While Zuckerberg is not universally liked or

A Questionable Source?

While the movie *The Social Network* has been popular, many critics wonder just how accurate it is. The movie is based on Ben Mezrich's book *The Accidental Billionaires*, and Mezrich begins the book with this note:

I do employ the technique of re-created dialogue. I have based this dialogue on the recollections of participants of the substance of conversations. Some of the conversations recounted in this book took place over long periods of time, in multiple locations, and thus some conversations and scenes were re-created and compressed. Rather than spread these conversations out, I sometimes set these scene in likely settings.[4]

This technique, along with the fact that Mezrich had few sources in his bibliography, did not footnote material, and did not have Zuckerberg's cooperation, have made critics skeptical about how truthful the book and movie are in their portrayal of both Zuckerberg and the events that led to the creation of Facebook. Mezrich himself claims, "There's a whole cabal of old-school journalists who hate the way I write nonfiction. It's a true story, but I write in a cinematic, thriller-esque style. It's a valid form of nonfiction."[5]

disliked, he is admired for what he has achieved at such a young age.

What Is Facebook?

Facebook is the creation that gave Zuckerberg his fame. Zuckerberg created Facebook as a way for people to communicate by sharing information, photographs, and links online via their specific Facebook identity and profile page. Users create a profile page with personal information, photographs of themselves and their families, employment information, and anything else they want to share with their friends. Then they can "friend" other people, allowing those friends access to both their personal information and the posts and status updates they make on Facebook. This kind of Web-based sharing is known as social networking and includes sites such as Facebook, MySpace, and Twitter. Users of these sites can connect with their friends as well as stay in touch with popular culture or current events. While some people question the effect social networking sites are having on individuals and cultures, the practice is spreading every year.

Advertisers love social networking sites because they allow marketing by word of mouth as people "like" products and share that information with their friends. Many companies, musical groups, or products actually have their own Facebook pages. Users can "like" these pages and become fans of them. Social networking sites are a great way for advertisers to promote their products because they can reach many people every day. As of January 2011, Facebook was approaching 600 million members from all over the world. Together, these users spend a total of more than 700 billion minutes on Facebook every month. As *Time* magazine explained in a 2010 article about Zuckerberg:

> *In less than seven years, Zuckerberg wired together a twelfth of humanity into a single network, thereby creating a social entity almost twice as large as the US. If Facebook*

Not a Popular Choice

Time magazine's choice of Zuckerberg as its Person of the Year created a storm of protest from those who felt that some of the other possible choices were more worthwhile. Many users thought Julian Assange, creator of a site called WikiLeaks, which has released hundreds of sensitive US government documents for public scrutiny, would be a better choice. *Time* readers were invited to vote on their choice for the title, but in the end, *Time* awarded the honor to Zuckerberg, even though voters overwhelmingly chose Assange. Some felt that *Time* was under political pressure from the Pentagon to not award the title to Assange.

*Facebook is popular with many age groups.
There are even classes that teach people
who are more than 60 years old how to use Facebook.*

were a country it would be the third largest, behind only China and India.[6]

Zuckerberg himself sums up his own goal for Facebook on his Facebook profile page: "I'm trying to make the world a more open place by helping people connect and share."[7]

SOMETHING FOR EVERYONE

Facebook has come a long way since its conception in 2004. Beginning in a college dormitory room, where Zuckerberg put together a Web site of students' faces and invited comments on them, it has grown and evolved quickly into a social networking site that is easy to use and popular among many ages. Adults often use Facebook to connect with people they may not see often or have lost touch with. Most teenagers use it as a way to communicate with their friends instead of by e-mail or phone. Unlike its main rival, MySpace, Facebook has become a place where both users and advertisers feel comfortable sharing and marketing. Most of this growth is due to Zuckerberg, who controls Facebook and feels strongly about running the site his own way. As a result, he has created something that has defined a new kind of popular social communication. This new communication takes place on the Internet and has little to do with personal face-to-face interaction. As *Time* magazine noted:

Facebook has merged with the social fabric of American life, and not just American but human life: nearly half of all Americans have a Facebook account, but 70 percent of Facebook users live outside the US. It's a permanent fact of our global social reality. We have entered the Facebook age, and Mark Zuckerberg is the man who brought us here.[8]

Zuckerberg is uncomfortable talking about himself, even his successes. As a result, he has become somewhat mysterious. The public's image of him ranges from positive to negative, depending on where the information comes from. But no one can deny what he has accomplished at only 26 years of age. At a time when most people are still new to the working world and struggling to establish their professional lives, he is running a huge company and constantly thinking of ways to make it even better and more lucrative.

The Bad and Good Side

Although many people would consider the increased communication gained by social networking a positive outcome of the site, Facebook contributes to social ills as well. For example, one Facebook user's husband left her with two small children and no money after he initiated an affair through Facebook. However, when the woman's Facebook network of friends discovered what had happened, they banded together and contributed money to help her and her family. This incident demonstrates Facebook's power, both positive and negative. It also reveals how Facebook has expanded many people's social networks. Rather than limited to a small geographical location, Facebook users can make friends and stay in touch with people around the world.

**A New Way
to Communicate**

It used to be that Internet users spent most of their time online using e-mail. But by March 2009, the Nielsen Company research firm announced that, for the first time, users were spending more time on social networks than they were on e-mail.

Many wonder how Zuckerberg created Facebook in such a short amount of time, and at such a young age. When he sat in his Harvard dorm room one night and thought of a prank to play on his classmates, he did not know that it would lead to creating something that would change the way humans communicate with each other. ⌐

Person *of the* **Year**

TIME

DECEMBER 27, 2010 / JANUARY

Facebook's
Mark
Zuckerberg
THE CONNECTOR

*Zuckerberg was on the cover of Time magazine
after being chosen as Time magazine's Person of the Year in 2010.*

Long before he created Facebook,
Mark was an intelligent and creative child.

BIRTH OF A
COMPUTER GENIUS

s *Time* magazine said in its article
about Mark, "[He] is part of the last
generation of human beings who will remember life
before the Internet, though only just."[1] Mark was
born in Dobbs Ferry, New York, on May 14, 1984.

His father, Edward, was a dentist, and his mother, Karen, had worked as a psychiatrist before quitting to help Edward in his dentistry office. Mark grew up with three sisters, Randi, Donna, and Arielle. His older sister Randi later became head of marketing for Facebook.

Mark grew up in a household that supported and encouraged him and his sisters. His father remembered:

> *[Mark] was strong-willed and relentless. For some kids, their questions could be answered with a simple yes or no. For Mark, if he asked for something, yes by itself would work, but no required much more. If you were going to say no to him you had better be prepared with a strong argument backed by facts, experiences, logic, reasons.*[2]

Family Fun

When they were children, Mark and his sisters loved to play pranks on each other. Mark and Randi pulled one prank on New Year's Eve of 1999 that was particularly memorable for Mark. At that time, everyone was worried about Y2K. Y2K was the theory that a glitch in computer date programming would destroy many of the computerized systems of the world when the year turned to 2000. Knowing that their parents were worried about Y2K, Mark and Randi waited until exactly midnight and then shut down the power in their house, making their parents think the Y2K fears had actually come true.

The Zuckerberg children were also creative. During one winter vacation, they decided to film a parody of the *Star Wars* movies called *The Star Wars Sill-ogy*. As Randi recalled:

> We took our job very seriously. Every morning we'd wake up and have production meetings. Mark's voice hadn't changed yet, so he played Luke Skywalker with a really high, squeaky voice, and then my little sister, who I think was 2, we stuck her in a garbage can as R2D2 and had her walk around.[3]

COMMUNICATING WITH COMPUTERS

Very early on, Mark had a knack for computer programming. By the

The Millennium Bug

Also known as the Millennium Bug, the Year 2000 Problem, and the Y2K Bug, Y2K was a projected computer and data-storage error that resulted from the practice of using only two digits to represent a year. It was feared that when the year 2000 arrived, computers would read it as 1900, not 2000. This would result in widespread computer failures and affect the infrastructure of the world. Companies and organizations worked hard to check, fix, and upgrade their computer systems. The actual problems projected for Y2K never appeared on any wide scale.

Mark's older sister Randi became head of marketing at Facebook.

time he was in middle school, he was already using computers and writing software for them. Edward was one of the first dentists to use digital radiography, so the house and office were filled with computers. Edward taught Mark Atari BASIC, a program for the Atari gaming system that allowed users to create their own basic computer programs.

Then, Mark moved on to more complicated programming.

Soon, Edward hired David Newman, a software developer, to tutor his 11-year-old son in computer programming. Newman said that Mark was a computer prodigy. It was actually difficult for Newman to keep ahead of Mark because he learned so quickly.

By the time he was 13 years old, Mark had created a basic computer network for his family that he called ZuckNet. Mark got the idea for the network when his dad explained that he wished there was a better way for the receptionist in the dental office to announce a patient's arrival, other than yelling. ZuckNet allowed the computers in the family home and his father's dental office to send messages to each other by pinging. Ping was a basic Internet program that allowed a user to verify that a particular Internet address existed and could accept

Randi Zuckerberg

Before becoming Facebook's director of marketing development, Mark's sister Randi attended Harvard. She studied psychology. Graduating in 2003, she went on to work for an advertising agency in New York City and then for Forbes before her brother convinced her to work for Facebook.

requests. It made a ping, a sound, when the message was received.

The receptionist would ping Dr. Zuckerberg when a patient arrived, and, at home, the children pinged each other. Mark's sister Randi explained the importance of ZuckNet for Mark, saying, "It was the first example of when he started building things—and he never stopped."[4] Mark's creation was a very primitive version of America Online (AOL) Instant Messenger, which came out the following year. Facebook would also later have an instant messaging feature.

Mark also began creating computer games. "I had a bunch of friends who were artists," he told Jose Antonio Vargas in a *New Yorker* magazine interview. "They'd come over, draw stuff, and I'd build a game out of it."[5] He also developed a computer version of the game Monopoly based on his middle school

Color Blind

One reason the dominant color on Facebook is blue is because Zuckerberg suffers from something called red-green color blindness. This means he has trouble telling the difference between the colors red and green. He sees blue better than other colors.

and a version of the game Risk based on the Roman Empire.

Soon after, Edward enrolled his son in a graduate computer course at a nearby college. According to Vargas:

> When his father dropped him off at the first class, the instructor looked at Edward and said, pointing to Mark, "You can't bring him to the classroom with you." Edward told the instructor that his son was the student.[6]

PHILLIPS EXETER ACADEMY

Mark attended Ardsley High School in Ardsley, New York, for two years. There, he studied classics before transferring to Phillips Exeter Academy, a preparatory school in Exeter, New Hampshire, for his junior year. He studied classical studies as well as won prizes for math, astronomy, and physics and was captain of the fencing team.

For his senior project at Phillips Exeter, Mark and another student wrote a music program called Synapse. Synapse used artificial intelligence to analyze a user's music listening habits and used that information to recommend other music. The program was posted online and received so many favorable reviews that both AOL and Microsoft offered to buy Synapse for around $1 million. They also wanted to hire Mark to develop it, but he would have had to drop out of school, so he refused.

GOING TO COLLEGE

Instead of dropping out of school to work, Mark decided to attend Harvard University in Cambridge, Massachusetts. He would study psychology and computer science. He already had a reputation as a computer

A Visit to Phillips Exeter

In January 2007, Mark made a presentation at his old school Phillips Exeter, according to the campus newspaper, *Lion's Eye*:

Mark Zuckerberg stopped off at Exeter on his way to the World Economic Forum in Davos, Switzerland. It is a rare assembly speaker who is as close in age to current Exonians as is Zuckerberg. . . . Zuckerberg told stories about Exeter, Harvard and his foray into the world of high-tech business. Throughout his talk, he emphasized the value of open information flow and on finding creative ways around obstacles. "This is how you can achieve revolutionary results," he suggested. Facebook is a dramatic example of such results.

After Assembly, Zuckerberg met in the Latin Study with a group of students. He was peppered with questions about how Facebook would change as more and more of its subscribers graduated from college and joined the work world, if he was influenced by competitors' sites and what kind of growth he predicted for the company. . . . One student wondered about the largest number of Facebook "friends" any subscriber has ever had (50,000) and another asked how many Zuckerberg has (300). One enterprising Exonian even inquired, "Is Facebook hiring?"[7]

programming prodigy. Mark moved into his dorm at Harvard. Little did he know that his time at Harvard would change not only his life but the lives of millions of people all over the world as well. ⌐

Mark attended Phillips Exeter Academy in New Hampshire.

In The Social Network, *actor Jesse Eisenberg plays Zuckerberg.*

HARVARD

There are conflicting viewpoints about Zuckerberg's years at Harvard University. In October 2010, the movie *The Social Network*, based on the book *The Accidental Billionaires* by Ben Mezrich, premiered in the United States. It tells the story of

Zuckerberg's years at Harvard and the founding of Facebook. The film portrays him as both a genius and as someone who was always angry, socially handicapped, and desperate to find a way into the social elite at Harvard. However, Zuckerberg claims he never really wanted to be part of the social clubs at Harvard and did not use his computer skills just to impress women.

Zuckerberg arrived at Harvard in the fall of 2002. He joined a Jewish fraternity, Alpha Epsilon Pi. There, at a party one Friday night, he met Priscilla Chan, a Chinese American from Boston. The two would later begin dating. Chan later described her first impressions of Zuckerberg: "He was this nerdy guy who was just a little bit out there."[1]

Regardless of whether Zuckerberg was an angry social climber or just a regular guy who was not heavily involved in the college social scene, he was always a good programmer. He could create software that was simple, yet addictive. At the beginning of his sophomore year, he created Course Match. The program enabled users to decide what college courses they wanted to take based on what other students at their school were choosing. It also allowed students to see who else might be in a given class, which would help them decide if they wanted to be in that same class. According to David Kirkpatrick in his book *The Facebook Effect*, "The status-conscious students at Harvard felt very differently about a class depending on who was in it."[2]

Zuckerberg installed a huge whiteboard in the hallway of his dormitory suite and used it to brainstorm with symbols and codes for software. One of his roommates, Dustin Moskovitz, recalled, "He really loved that whiteboard. He always wanted to draw out his ideas, even when that didn't necessarily make them clearer."[3]

FACEMASH

The success of Course Match led Zuckerberg to a new idea, although this one was more like the pranks he used to play as a child. He invented Facemash, a program with the purpose of figuring out who was the most attractive person on campus. He used the same kind of computer code that was used to rank chess players. Users simply compared pictures of two people of the same sex and decided which one was better looking. As that person's ranking got higher, they were compared to other high-ranking people.

Zuckerberg created Facebook when he was a college student at Harvard University in Cambridge, Massachusetts.

However, in a blog journal that Zuckerberg kept at the time, it appears that he launched the program because he was upset about a specific girl. He wrote, "I need to think of something to make to take my mind off her."[4] In the blog, he also considered comparing students' faces to farm animals, but this did not appear in the final version of the program.

Zuckerberg finished the entire program in just eight hours, ending at 4:00 a.m. on October 28, 2003. Getting all the photographs to use on Facemash was not too difficult for Zuckerberg. Every house, or dorm, at Harvard where undergraduates lived had something called a facebook. Facebooks consisted of the pictures taken of every student the day they arrived at Harvard, to enable students to get to know each other. Most of the photos were awkward and unflattering, but Zuckerberg found a way to get the

Stats Class

Zuckerberg's suite mate and Facebook cofounder Moskovitz actually wrote a paper for his statistics class about social networks and colleges during the spring after the launching of Facebook. Many people feel Facebook's ultimate success came from the fact that it began at a college, where people have the densest social networks and socialize more than at any other time in their lives.

Moskovitz used data from the new site for his paper, where he argued that any student on campus is within two degrees of any other student on campus. This means that there is, on average, only one intermediate relationship between any two people on campus. Moskovitz got an A in the class he wrote the paper for, which he recalls as being pretty good considering that most of his time that semester was spent working on Zuckerberg's new site. He also felt that Facebook succeeded because Harvard was an environment where students were always starting Web sites and other business endeavors. There were plenty of resources available for developing any business, including money to invest in new projects, thanks to the fact that many Harvard students came from wealthy and influential families.

digital versions of these photographs from nine of the 12 houses. He simply hacked into the directories via the Internet or downloaded them directly from the house's Ethernet.

Facemash was up and running on November 2, 2003. The home page said, "Were we let in [to Harvard] for our looks? No. Will we be judged by them? Yes."[5] Zuckerberg sent the link to a few of his friends, supposedly just to test it, but soon word spread and Facemash was an instant hit on campus. Harvard's newspaper, the *Harvard Crimson*, commented on the new site:

> *[Zuckerberg is] catering to the worst side of Harvard students . . . we Harvard students could indulge our fondness for judging those around us on superficial criteria without ever having to face any of the judged in person.*[6]

The site drew so much attention that Zuckerberg's laptop, which

Zuckerberg's Suite Mates

The other students who lived in the small suite H33 at Harvard's Kirkland House with Zuckerberg would also become the basis of Facebook's first team. Chris Hughes was a literature and history major who was interested in public policy issues, Moskovitz was an economics major, and Billy Olson was involved in theater. Olson would have little to do with Facebook, although he did contribute initial ideas to Facemash. Moskovitz and Hughes would help build Facebook into the social networking giant it became, although they ultimately did not remain with the company.

Disciplined

After the launch of Facemash, Zuckerberg was called before Harvard University's Administrative Board, along with Billy Olson and Joe Green, who had helped with the site. While Zuckerberg was given probation and made to see a counselor for his violations of security, copyright, and privacy, the other two were not punished. Zuckerberg probably would have received a harsher punishment if he had included farm animal comparisons on the Facemash site, an idea he toyed with but ultimately rejected.

hosted the site, kept freezing up. But after protests from students and women's groups on campus, the university shut down Zuckerberg's Internet access. By that time, 450 students had already visited the site and voted on 22,000 pairs of photographs. The site had only been open from mid-afternoon on November 2 to 10:30 that evening.

Zuckerberg was disciplined by the university, put on probation, and ordered to see a counselor and apologize to the women's groups— Fuerza Latina and the Association of Harvard Black Women—that had complained about the site. Zuckerberg had learned a valuable lesson from the Facemash episode: people love to use the Internet for social interaction. This realization would eventually lead to the birth of Facebook.

*Zuckerberg's Facemash Web site
would lead to something even bigger—Facebook.*

Zuckerberg helped, left to right, Tyler Winklevoss, Divya Narendra, and Cameron Winklevoss with a Web site called Harvard Connection.

THE BIRTH OF FACEBOOK

fter the success of Facemash, Zuckerberg continued to work on a variety of programming projects. He said,

> I had this hobby of just building these little projects. I had like twelve projects that year. Of course I wasn't fully committed

to any one of them. [Most of them were about] seeing how people were connected through mutual references.[1]

That was a theme that would run through most of Zuckerberg's projects and eventually led to the birth of the biggest social networking site, and his biggest success—Facebook.

One of the little projects Zuckerberg worked on was helping three Harvard seniors build a Web site. The three men—twin brothers Cameron and Tyler Winklevoss and their friend Divya Narendra—had an idea to construct an Internet dating and socializing site called Harvard Connection. They saw it as a way to not only bring Harvard students together but to also tell them about parties and nightclubs and other things to do. The men were not computer programmers, so after reading about Zuckerberg and Facemash in the *Harvard Crimson*, they asked him if he would do the programming for their new service.

The Six Degrees Program

One of the little programs that Zuckerberg developed while at Harvard was a tribute to a favorite computer science professor. Called Six Degrees of Harry Lewis, it created a fun network of connections to Lewis based on relationships that Zuckerberg gleaned from issues of the *Harvard Crimson*. Users could type in any Harvard student's name and the program would tell them how that student was connected to Lewis.

Zuckerberg helped the three men with their site for a few weeks, but eventually he abandoned their project to pursue one of his own. This decision, as well as some incriminating instant messages about Zuckerberg's intentions toward the Harvard Connection group, would later have legal repercussions. But at the time, Zuckerberg was simply moving on to his own project, one that he had a personal stake in.

TheFacebook.com

In January 2004, Zuckerberg paid $35 to register the domain name TheFacebook.com for a period of one year. He was creating a new site—one that took some elements from Course Match and Facemash, as well as a service called Friendster. Friendster was one of the first social networking sites where people posted their profiles and linked to other people, primarily for dating. Friendster had been very popular on campus before the number of users nationwide made it unwieldy and slow. Some Harvard students also used a new networking service called MySpace, though it had not yet taken off.

Zuckerberg already knew how popular his Facemash program had been, and many students wanted to see online versions of the facebooks that Harvard printed and distributed to incoming students. Harvard's administration was slow to pursue this idea, but students and the *Harvard Crimson* kept pushing it. Zuckerberg decided to build one himself.

The key issue the college had with an online facebook was legal issues concerning privacy of the students' information. The problem with Facemash had been that students did not get to decide whether their photographs were uploaded. An editorial in the *Harvard Crimson* stated, "Much

Friendster and MySpace

Friendster and MySpace were two very popular social networking sites that preceded Facebook. Friendster was the first site that allowed users to meet people in a virtual alternative to real-life face-to-face introductions and operated by connecting friends and friends of friends to each other. It also allowed people to share musical groups, hobbies, and other interests. However, today, most of Friendster's traffic is in Asia, and the site has declined sharply in popularity since 2005.

MySpace was founded as a site specifically oriented to bands and other musical groups who were often not permitted on Friendster, allowing them to create pages and advertise themselves. Until April 2008, when it was overtaken by Facebook, MySpace was the most popular social networking site. However, MySpace has often come under fire because, since users are not required to join under their real identities, sexual predators have used it to entice younger users, stalkers have used it to pursue their victims, and the software is vulnerable to spyware programs. In 2008, MySpace launched a music download business that it hoped would rival iTunes.

of the trouble surrounding the Facemash could have been eliminated if only the site had limited itself to students who voluntarily uploaded their own photos."[2] Zuckerberg later claimed that it was this editorial that gave him the initial idea for TheFacebook.com.

Zuckerberg did not intend to create a dating site but, instead, a reliable directory of Harvard students based on real information:

> *Our project just started off as a way to help people share more at Harvard. . . . so people could see more of what's going on at school. I wanted to make it so I could get access to information about anyone, and anyone could share anything that they wanted to.*[3]

Zuckerberg also seemed to be aware that this particular programming project might be more serious than his previous ones. He made a deal with a classmate named Eduardo

From Laptop to Server

One of the problems Zuckerberg had with the Facemash program was that it operated from his laptop and over the Harvard network. The popularity of the site made the laptop crash, losing data. And the use of the Harvard network enabled the school to shut down the site at will. So, as Zuckerberg developed TheFacebook.com, he paid an online hosting service $85 a month to host his new Web site. Not only would it protect his own computer, but it also allowed the site to operate independently of the Harvard computer network. In this way, Zuckerberg could maintain control.

Saverin, giving him one-third ownership in TheFacebook.com. In exchange, Saverin provided a small investment of cash and his help with business aspects of the site.

The Launch

On February 4, 2004, TheFacebook.com went live. The home page read:

> *Thefacebook is an online directory that connects people though social networks at college. We have opened up Thefacebook for popular consumption at Harvard University. You can use Thefacebook to: Search for people at your school; Find out who are in your classes; Look up your friends' friends; See a visualization of your social network.*[4]

The site spread more quickly than anyone could have imagined, as people e-mailed their friends to join. Only four days after the site launched, it already had 650

Eduardo Saverin

Saverin, an original investor in Facebook and one of Zuckerberg's first partners, is the son of a wealthy Brazilian businessman. He is said to be a math genius and belonged to the same fraternity at Harvard as Zuckerberg. He was also a member of the university's Investment Club and a great chess player. Much of Mezrich's book about the founding of Facebook, *The Accidental Billionaires*, is written from Saverin's perspective. Saverin was willing to collaborate with him. Zuckerberg, on the other hand, refused to work with Mezrich.

members, and 300 more joined the next day. The
site was limited to people who had a Harvard e-mail
address and users had to provide their real names.
But users could also decide who they wanted to be
able to see their information.

Although students, and alumni and faculty,
initially used TheFacebook for social purposes,
people also soon found it useful for things such
as organizing study groups and posting notices
about activities and parties. It also still contained
information about courses, much like Course Match
had. Zuckerberg was careful to emphasize that he did
not create the site with the idea of making money. To
him, making the Web site fun was more important
than making money with it, and that motivation
would continue as TheFacebook.com grew.

More Schools

Soon, students from other colleges were asking
to be included in TheFacebook. As the site grew,
Zuckerberg realized he would need more help to
maintain it and employed his roommate Moskovitz
to help. Soon, the site was opened to students
at Columbia, Stanford, and Yale Universities.
Soon, more and more people wanted to interview

First only available to Harvard students, professors, and alumni, TheFacebook quickly gained popularity and was opened to other colleges.

Zuckerberg, who disliked doing interviews and talking in public. Zuckerberg eventually hired his roommate Hughes to be TheFacebook's spokesman.

Other Facebooks

Although TheFacebook kept adding colleges and universities, it was often not the first online social network on many campuses. At Columbia University, a community site called CUCommunity launched a month before TheFacebook, and in just four weeks, it had 1,900 users. It would be months before TheFacebook overtook CUCommunity in popularity. Yale University had YaleStation, another networking site that had fewer features than The-Facebook but was still immensely popular with students.

TheFacebook.com had been in operation for just one month, but it already had 10,000 active users. What started as a project that Zuckerberg created for fun was quickly turning into a real business. It consumed most of Zuckerberg's time. At the end of his sophomore year, he moved to California for the summer, assuming he would be back at Harvard in the fall. However, Zuckerberg would drop out of school that summer.

Zuckerberg's social networking site was a hit only a month after it launched.

Sean Parker

INTO THE REAL WORLD

y June 2004, Zuckerberg had been offered $10 million for his new company by investors who were amazed at how quickly TheFacebook.com was growing. He was only 20 years old, and the site had been running for just four months. But Zuckerberg refused offers to buy TheFacebook.com.

DEVELOPING FACEBOOK

Zuckerberg rented a house in Palo Alto, California, intending to stay there for just the summer and convinced many of his friends to come with him. There, they worked on TheFacebook. During his first few weeks in California, Zuckerberg ran into Sean Parker, who was known for his creation of the music-sharing site Napster. Parker and Zuckerberg had met previously in New York, but now Parker became part of TheFacebook.com. He had a great deal of experience with the Internet and also introduced Zuckerberg to many Silicon Valley investors. Parker later remembered one of his first conversations with Zuckerberg:

> *He was not thinking, "Let's make some money and get out." This wasn't like a*

Silicon Valley

Silicon Valley is a nickname for an area of California located in the southern San Francisco Bay region. Originally, it was home to companies that produced the silicon microchips needed by the computer industry. The area also attracted investors who wanted to put money into the new and growing technology industry. Even today, when technology companies are no longer enjoying amazing growth, it is seen as the center of high-tech research and development companies.

get-rich-quick scheme. This was "Let's build something that has lasting cultural value and try to take over the world." But he didn't know what that meant. [1]

Parker was an important addition to TheFacebook, especially when it came to talking to investors and other business-deal situations. Parker had experience with these types of conversations, while Zuckerberg was still uncomfortable with them. Parker found a lawyer for TheFacebook team. Parker would become the president of TheFacebook from 2004 to 2005.

The group spent the summer of 2004 bolstering TheFacebook.com site for the fall, when it was expected that even more colleges and students would be joining. Zuckerberg had already made the decision not to return to Harvard. He knew his career would involve the Internet because of its growing popularity.

Parker and Napster

Parker is best known as the creator—along with fellow student Shawn Fanning—of an online music file sharing site called Napster. Operating from 1999 to 2001, Napster allowed users to share their MP3 music files with each other, rather than having to purchase their music in traditional ways. However, Napster was charged by the music industry with infringing on copyrights and was shut down by a court order in July of 2001.

He and his friends often talked about the trends in technology and the Internet. "Isn't it obvious that everyone [is] going to be on the Internet?" Zuckerberg said. "Isn't it, like, inevitable that there would be a huge social network of people? It was something that we expected to happen."[2]

Companies continued to be interested in buying TheFacebook. Executives from search engine giant Google made an offer for the site, but Zuckerberg did not want to relinquish control to such a large company. He felt his site was about

Serendipity

One of the reasons Facebook is so popular, particularly with older users, is the concept of serendipity, as Zuckerberg describes in an interview:

We have this concept of serendipity— humans do. A lucky coincidence. It's like you go to a restaurant and you bump into a friend that you haven't seen for a while. That's awesome. That's serendipitous. And a lot of the reason why that seems so magical is because it doesn't happen often. But I think the reality is that those circumstances aren't actually rare. It's just that we probably miss like 99% of it.[3]

Zuckerberg's interviewer, Lev Grossman, added:

Facebook wants to . . . turn the lonely, antisocial world of random chance into a friendly world, a serendipitous world. You'll be working and living inside a network of people, and you'll never have to be alone again. The Internet, and the whole world, will feel more like a family, or a college dorm, or an office where your co-workers are also your best friends.[4]

people, while Google was about data. If he wanted to keep control, he would need to stay independent.

An Eye toward Growth

Even in 2004, Zuckerberg assumed TheFacebook was going to keep growing. He attempted to stay one step ahead of it, always planning for future growth. The servers that powered the site were located in Santa Clara, California, and the group frequently needed to go there and add more servers. Zuckerberg was obsessed with preventing a slowdown or an outage, which was partly what made the site Friendster lose its popularity.

But all this expansion cost money. TheFacebook was no longer running on the $85 a month hosting fee. Now, the company was paying for servers and employees' salaries. Much of the money for the site came out of a bank account Saverin and Zuckerberg had started. This led to problems between Saverin and the company, which would later cause larger legal problems for Zuckerberg.

In 2005, Zuckerberg's company purchased the new domain name Facebook.com and dropped "the" from the site's title. The site also expanded its advertising by allowing companies to buy advertising

*Google wanted to buy TheFacebook,
but Zuckerberg turned down the offer.*

space on pages as well as create their own company-
specific pages. Zuckerberg was determined that
the site should be able to pay its own costs. He and

Parker also continued to find investors to fund the site's growth.

By 2006, Facebook had approximately 7 million users, so Parker and Zuckerberg decided the site should go beyond simply serving college students. They felt that Facebook was ready to become a rival to MySpace. But their attempts to attract high school students were not wildly successful at first. Even as bigger companies offered to buy Facebook, some people wondered if the site had already peaked in popularity.

AN OFFER?

In 2006, Yahoo!, another Internet company, offered to buy Facebook for $1 billion in cash. An offer like that seemed impossible to resist, and Zuckerberg made a verbal agreement to sell the site. Yahoo! had millions of users, but it was having trouble establishing a social networking presence. Facebook, on the other hand, had the tools and the setup but needed to keep attracting users. It seemed like a good fit.

But the timing turned out to be bad. Just after Zuckerberg agreed to sell, Yahoo! announced that its sales and earnings would be slower than previously projected and its new advertising features would be delayed. According to Fred Vogelstein in his article on Wired.com,

> [Yahoo!'s] stock price plunged 22 percent overnight. Terry Semel, Yahoo!'s CEO at the time, reacted by cutting his offer [for Facebook] from $1 billion to $800 million. Zuckerberg, who had been warned about Semel's reputation for last-minute renegotiations, walked away. Two months later, Semel reissued the original $1 billion bid, but by then Zuckerberg had convinced his board and executive team that Yahoo! wasn't a serious partner and that Facebook would be worth more on its own. He rejected the offer and became famous as the cocky youngster who turned down $1 billion.[5]

Zuckerberg's girlfriend, Priscilla Chan, looked back at that period in time as the most stressful of Zuckerberg's life. Although many people could not believe he would

Wirehog

One of Zuckerberg's projects, when he first arrived in California, was a file-sharing service called Wirehog. Launched in 2004, it allowed users to share music, video and text files, as well as any other kind of digital information with their friends. It was directly connected to Facebook, essentially turning a user's friends into sources of content. However, Parker feared that Wirehog had the potential for involving Facebook in the same kind of copyright lawsuits that shut down Napster. In 2006, Zuckerberg gave up on Wirehog.

In 2006, after months of negotiations,
Zuckerberg turned down a $1 billion offer from Yahoo!.

turn down such a lucrative offer, critics would
admit that Facebook is now worth much more than
Yahoo!'s offer and Zuckerberg did the right thing.

The Social Graph

Having decided to keep Facebook under his
control, Zuckerberg focused on accomplishing
his own goals for the site. He wanted to create an

online graph that would show the interconnected webs of people's relationships in the real world. While many social networks helped their users create new identities and link to new people, Zuckerberg did not want Facebook to be about making new friends. "People already have their friends, acquaintances, and business connections," Zuckerberg explained. "So rather than building new connections, what we are doing is just mapping them out."[6]

Three things would have to happen in order for Zuckerberg to map this social graph. He would need to make it easier for friends to communicate with each other. He would need to extend Facebook's membership to everyone in the world. He would need to open the site to software developers who could build new applications to keep users coming back to the site. However, the ways Zuckerberg attempted to achieve

Toddler CEO

In 2007, Kara Swisher, who writes the Internet blog *All Things Digital*, called Zuckerberg a "toddler CEO" and felt he was too young and inexperienced to run a company as big as Facebook.[7] But in a 2010 interview with Lesley Stahl on the CBS television show *60 Minutes*, Swisher said she now knows Zuckerberg is actually a prodigy and is running the company quite well.

these goals would bring some of the first protests from his Facebook users. But users were not the only ones complaining about Facebook and Zuckerberg: two very big lawsuits would soon occupy much of Zuckerberg's attention.

Zuckerberg had a clear vision in his mind
of what kind of Web site Facebook would be.

Despite its success, Zuckerberg's Facebook also suffered difficulties, including legal struggles.

THE HARVARD CONNECTION LAWSUIT

s Facebook continued to grow, Zuckerberg found himself embroiled in a lawsuit that stemmed from his Harvard days and the Harvard Connection Web site. In late 2003, Zuckerberg allegedly had spent some time helping three of his Harvard classmates—Tyler and Cameron Winklevoss and Divya Narendra—launch a social networking and dating site called Harvard Connection. Zuckerberg claimed he stopped programming it for them when he realized it was not likely to succeed. David Kirkpatrick, who carefully researched Facebook's history through interviews with Zuckerberg and his cofounders, offers his version of the story in *The Facebook Effect*,

> *Zuckerberg worked off and on writing code for Harvard Connection. After a few weeks he appeared to have lost interest, though he apparently didn't make that clear to the Winklevosses and Narendra. They began to complain that he was taking too long.*[1]

The three men had additional ideas for the site. They wanted it to include a list of nightclubs that would offer discounts to registered Harvard Connection users. They also wanted a feature that would project how close the user's interests were to the interests of other users, and use that in creating dating recommendations.

But Zuckerberg was continuing to lose interest in the site, writing in an e-mail, "I'm still a little skeptical that we have enough functionality in the site to really draw the attention and gain the critical mass necessary to get a site like this to run."[2] On January 14, 2004, he told them he no longer had time to work on the project.

THEFT?

But as Facebook launched and began to grow exponentially in popularity, the three Harvard Connection creators claimed that Zuckerberg stole many ideas for Facebook from their ideas. Narendra said he and the Winklevosses had the idea for Harvard Connection in December 2002, long before Facemash and TheFacebook existed.

TheFacebook launched in February 2004, and six days

The Winklevoss Twins

Cameron and Tyler Winklevoss were born in Southampton, New York, on August 21, 1981. They are mirror-image twins, making one left-handed and one right-handed, and they have always worked together on projects. At only 13 years old, the twins taught themselves HTML computer coding and started a business to build Web sites for other businesses. Both brothers participated in rowing at Harvard and later competed in the 2008 Olympics in Beijing, finishing in sixth place.

In spring of 2005, the twins were evicted from an apartment they shared in Cambridge, Massachusetts, because of noise and a fight that took place on the property and failure to pay rent. The twins retaliated by creating a fake Web site for the apartment complex on which they posted defamatory content. The apartment complex sued them in 2005, and the twins settled two days later for an undisclosed amount of money.

later, Cameron Winklevoss made his first claim that Zuckerberg had misappropriated work he had done for Harvard Connection and used it to launch TheFacebook. He sent an e-mail to Zuckerberg:

> It has come to our attention (Tyler, Divya and myself) that you have launched a website named TheFacebook.com. Prior to this launch, we entered into an agreement with you under which you would help us develop our proprietary website (HarvardConnection) and do so in a timely manner. . . .
>
> Over the last three months . . . you stalled the development of our website, while you were developing your own website in unfair competition with ours, and without our knowledge or agreement. . . . At this time we have notified our counsel and are prepared to take action.[3]

The Winklevosses appealed to the Harvard Administration Board. Zuckerberg wrote a letter in response,

Guest of a Guest

Cameron Winklevoss now publishes a blog called *Guest of a Guest*. It focuses on social activities and nightlife in Los Angeles, the Hamptons, and New York.

explaining his side. Zuckerberg asserted that the Harvard Connection men had been frustrating to work with and that he was "appalled" they were now threatening him with a lawsuit because, Zuckerberg said, Harvard Connection and TheFacebook were "completely different."[4]

A Lawsuit

TheFacebook and Harvard Connection—which eventually launched in late spring of 2004 as ConnectU—were different. ConnectU was mostly about dating and making deals with promoters, while TheFacebook was intended to replace printed facebooks.

However, the difference did not stop the Winklevoss brothers and Narendra from filing a lawsuit against Zuckerberg in the fall of 2004. The lawsuit claimed Zuckerberg had breached his contract, stolen ideas, and engaged in unfair business practices.

*In the Harvard Connection lawsuit,
Zuckerberg was accused of stealing the idea for Facebook.*

The three men wanted to be part of TheFacebook company and be paid damages equal to its value. As Cameron Winklevoss stated, "[Zuckerberg] stole the moment, he stole the idea, and he stole the execution."[6] The suit itself read, in part, that Zuckerberg stole ideas such as:

> creating the first niche social network for college/university students; serving as a directory of people and their interests and qualifications, a forum for the expression of opinions and ideas, and a safe network of connections.[7]

Unfortunately, some of the instant messages Zuckerberg sent during the time he was working for the Harvard Connection site were later released. In one message Zuckerberg was asked what he was going to do about the Harvard Connection Web site and allegedly responded that he was going to drop it and focus on getting his own site out first. Zuckerberg later said he regretted the messages and that something he said when he was 19 should not be used to judge him now.

Quinn Emanuel Lawsuit

The Winklevosses have been involved in other lawsuits besides their Facebook suit. Quinn Emanuel, one of the legal groups hired by ConnectU to fight Facebook, inadvertently released the amount of the Facebook settlement in its marketing material, an amount that was supposed to remain confidential. ConnectU filed a suit against the group for malpractice, but in 2010, an arbitration panel ruled that Quinn Emanuel had committed no malpractice and was still entitled to its $13 million legal fee.

The lawsuit, which was complicated by countersuits, was not settled until February 2008. The Winklevoss group would receive $20 million in cash and 1,253,326 shares of Facebook stock. However, in 2010 the three men tried to change the settlement, claiming they were misled about the value of the Facebook stock and that they were actually receiving less money than they were told due to fluctuations in Facebook's value. As of January 2011, the lawsuit continued to drag out.

EDUARDO SAVERIN

Meanwhile, Zuckerberg and cofounder Eduardo Saverin also had a falling out. Saverin was supposed to be the business leader of Facebook, but he had very little to do with the actual daily workings of the site and stayed in New York, while Facebook itself operated in California. In July 2004, Zuckerberg filed a

Chang Group Lawsuit

The Harvard Connection team joined forces with a group called i2hub, another peer-to-peer Internet service. They collaborated on several projects, but in 2009, Wayne Chang, i2hub's founder, filed a lawsuit against the Winklevosses seeking 50 percent of their Facebook settlement. Chang claimed he was not listed on a patent filed by the Winklevosses during the time he worked with them as a coinventor. As a partner in their company, he felt entitled to share in the Facebook settlement. As of January 2011, the lawsuit was not yet resolved.

lawsuit against Saverin, claiming he had frozen TheFacebook's bank accounts and jeopardized the company. Saverin filed his own suit, claiming it was his money that provided the start-up funds for TheFacebook, money that Zuckerberg never matched as he was supposed to. Saverin also claimed Zuckerberg used that money for his personal expenses. As a result of the suits, Zuckerberg transferred TheFacebook's property rights and membership interests to a new version of the TheFacebook company in Delaware, reducing the amount of stock Saverin had in the new company. Saverin was no longer considered an employee of TheFacebook.

Meanwhile, the social networking site continued to grow, and it remained largely under Zuckerberg's control. He would make decisions for the site that were not always popular, and conflicting stories about his personality and motivation would soon emerge.

Tyler, right, and Cameron Winklevoss claim that they did not sue Zuckerberg simply for money, but because they felt what he had done was immoral.

Zuckerberg thought the News Feed would be a great addition to Facebook. However, some users protested the change.

Fact and Fiction

Zuckerberg's vision for Facebook continued to develop. In September 2006, Facebook launched a new feature called News Feed. It basically meant anything users posted on Facebook, such as photographs, status updates, or groups they joined, would pop up on the News Feed page of all of their friends to see immediately. As one Facebook employee put it, "The Internet could help you answer a million questions, but not the most important one, the one you wake up with every day—'How are the people doing that I care about?'"[1] News Feed was activated on September 5, 2006, but with unexpected consequences.

It would be the biggest Facebook crisis that Zuckerberg had dealt with so far. Most of the users hated the new feature. Many were not expecting their activities to be broadcast so publicly to their networks and were surprised by the change. Soon, a group had formed called Students Against Facebook News Feed. At least 10 percent of the site's users were protesting the change. Nearly 500 protest groups eventually formed. One user from Students Against Facebook News Feed posted:

Ambient Intimacy

In 2007, technology expert Leisa Reichelt coined a new phrase: *ambient intimacy*. It describes the dynamics of Facebook and other social networking services that allow people to talk about themselves to groups or friends or followers. As she describes it, ambient intimacy is "being able to keep in touch with people with a level of regularity and intimacy that you wouldn't usually have access to, because time and space conspire to make it impossible."[2]

You went a bit too far this time, Facebook. Very few of us want everyone automatically knowing what we update . . . news feed is just too creepy, too stalker-esque, and a feature that has to go.[3]

But Zuckerberg had faith in News Feed. He responded to the users' concerns:

We agree, stalking isn't cool; but being able to know what's going on in your friends' lives is. This is information people used to dig for on a daily basis, nicely reorganized and summarized so people can learn about the people they care about. None of your information is visible to anyone who couldn't see it before the changes."[4]

THE PRIVACY ISSUE

Zuckerberg and his Facebook team eventually dealt with the uproar by adding controls to the site that allowed users to limit how much of their information could be seen and by whom. The incident pointed out a growing concern among Facebook users that perhaps Zuckerberg and Facebook were not concerned enough about user privacy.

Even after their experience with the News Feed feature, the Facebook team and Zuckerberg continued to make some decisions that worried users. Zuckerberg kept looking for new ways to make Facebook more than a social networking tool. He saw it as a prime place for advertisers, and on November 6, 2007, he unveiled a new Facebook program called Beacon. Beacon would enable advertisers to access a user's Facebook page. If that person bought something from that retailer's Web site, the purchase information would show up on the shopper's Facebook page as well as on his or her friends' pages. It showed the user's

Privacy and LinkedIn

One issue that continues to dog Facebook is that of privacy. The comfort level users have with the site and their privacy varies depending on the age of the user. Some adult users are often uncomfortable with the idea that one profile online should contain so much of their personal information. Many adults limit their Facebook friends to personal friends and not people they work with. Others might include everyone they know but limit how much personal information is available on their profile and use the site for networking. Some new sites, such as LinkedIn, were created to address this problem and provide a business networking platform.

LinkedIn creator Reid Hoffman, who invested in Facebook early on, commented on Zuckerberg and the privacy issue:

Mark doesn't believe that social and professional lives are distinct. That's a classic college student view. One of the things you learn as you get older is that you have these different contexts.[5]

Users have to decide for themselves how much privacy they need in both their personal lives and their professional lives, and how much overlap they feel comfortable with.

Zuckerberg gave a press conference presentation about Facebook's privacy settings on May 26, 2010.

Facebook friends anything he or she had purchased online, hoping people would note what their friends were buying and perhaps be persuaded to buy from that same site. It would also allow someone to post something for sale on a site such as eBay and automatically let the poster's Facebook friends know what the poster had for sale.

Again, users' Facebook accounts automatically used Beacon to share their purchases without warning them. People immediately complained about their buying habits being shared with everyone they had friended. Facebook was forced to make Beacon a utility that people had to choose to use first before it started sharing their purchases. However, many users still worried about the control the Facebook company had over their personal information and how it was shared with their Facebook friends.

THE REAL MARK ZUCKERBERG

The privacy issues surrounding Facebook brought up some of the first concerns about Zuckerberg's character. Mezrich's 2009 book, *The Accidental Billionaires*, took Zuckerberg's negative public persona further. Mezrich portrayed Zuckerberg during his Harvard years as socially awkward, angry, and seeking both girls and acceptance in his social circles. The movie *The Social Network*, which opened in 2010 and was based on Mezrich's book, perpetuated this view of Zuckerberg. Many wonder if these portrayals are accurate.

Zuckerberg and Facebook did not authorize the book and refused requests to speak with the makers of the movie. Zuckerberg later commented on the film,

> It's a movie. It's fun. A lot of it is fiction, but even the filmmakers will say that. They're trying to build a good story. This is my life so I know it's not that dramatic. . . . Maybe it would be fun to remember it as partying and all this crazy drama but who knows? Maybe it'll be an interesting story.[6]

So, who is the real Mark Zuckerberg? Jose Antonio Vargas, in his interview with Zuckerberg in September 2010, described him:

> His affect can be distant and disorienting, a strange mixture of shy and cocky. When he's not interested in what someone is talking about, he'll just look away and say "Yeah, yeah." The typical complaint about Zuckerberg is that he's "a robot." Indeed he sometimes talks like an Instant Message —brusque, flat as a dial tone—and he can come off as flip and condescending, as if he always knew something that you didn't. But face to face he is often charming, and he's becoming more comfortable onstage.[7]

Zuckerberg's reputation also took on a new depth in July 2010, when he attended a conference in Idaho and was seated next to the mayor of Newark, New Jersey, Cory Booker. As a result of that dinner, Zuckerberg announced on *The Oprah Winfrey Show* that he would contribute $100 million of his Facebook fortune, creating a foundation called Startup: Education. The foundation's first project would help the Newark school system. Zuckerberg explained,

> *Every child deserves a good education and right now that's not happening. I've had a lot of opportunities in my life and a lot of that comes from having gone to really good schools. And I want to do what I can to make sure everyone has those opportunities.*[8]

When critics commented on the fact that the announcement took place just weeks before the opening of *The Social Network*, Oprah said

The Dangers of Facebook

What many users, particularly younger ones, forget is that nothing posted on Facebook is ever really confidential, and even things that are deleted might not be gone forever. This can have negative repercussions. Facebook disclosures, such as photographs of users at parties or involved in pranks, can cause embarrassment or catch a user in a lie. However, the effects can be even worse. A 2009 poll found that 35 percent of US companies had rejected a job applicant because of information found on social networks.

Zuckerberg had wanted to remain anonymous, but she convinced him to appear on her show.

Despite privacy concerns and conflicting views of what Facebook's founder was really like, Facebook had continued to grow and evolve every year. In October 2007, after a public bidding war with Google, Microsoft Corporation made a $240 million investment in Facebook, giving Microsoft a 1.6 percent share in it. In 2008, Facebook cosponsored presidential debates with ABC News. Next, the site launched in Spanish, French, and German, and then added a translation application that would enable 21 more languages to be used on the site. Facebook was now global. ⌐

Zuckerberg, with Booker, explained how Startup: Education would use the Newark school system to show how other schools could be reformed.

Facebook headquarters in Palo Alto, California

Running Facebook

Facebook is a company that continues to
grow at a rapid pace and is always planning
for the future. As the company grew, Zuckerberg
needed to stay ahead. So he add more employees
to help Facebook focus on areas such as marketing,

advertising, and international growth. He also set up a Facebook headquarters.

HEADQUARTERS

Because running Facebook and keeping the site growing is basically most of what Zuckerberg spends his time doing, taking a tour of the Facebook headquarters helps in understanding Zuckerberg. Due to the fast pace of its growth, Facebook has had seven headquarters in seven years.

As of 2010, Facebook occupied two office buildings in Palo Alto located just a few minutes apart, but Zuckerberg was looking for a campus of buildings to hold the entire company. The company also had a facility in Santa Clara just for the enormous bank—tens of thousands—of servers that it takes to run the site. Facebook believed in multiple backups to keep the site

Hacking

The word *hack*—which is written as graffiti on the walls of Facebook's headquarters—does not always mean illegally accessing Internet information. Zuckerberg defines hacking as building something very quickly. Facebook is known for its all-night "hackathons" when engineers stay up all night to build a new feature. Zuckerberg participates in these hackathons, coding right along with everyone else.

running, even if there should be a power blackout in the area. The company made plans to build two more data centers in Oregon and North Carolina. The company also had sales offices in cities all over the United States and the world. As chief executive officer, Zuckerberg covers a lot of ground.

Whiteboards, Aquariums, and Employees

Despite the fact that it is a huge business, Facebook's headquarters reflect something of Zuckerberg's relaxed style. There are no private spaces, walls, or offices, just an open area scattered with desks. The only enclosed rooms are conference rooms, which have glass walls. One area holds a gaming system and controllers, and bikes and two-wheeled skateboards called Ripstiks are strewn everywhere. With glass walls and open workstations, the office space reflects the company's "open" philosophy.

The first employees of Facebook were all Zuckerberg's friends from Phillips Exeter and Harvard, but over the years, most of them have moved on to other enterprises. As the company grew and was forced to become more professional, many of Zuckerberg's friends felt uncomfortable working for a large company. Others felt that Zuckerberg was difficult to work for. One of his friends, Chris Hughes, commented,

> *Working with Mark is very challenging. You're never sure if what you're doing is something he likes or he doesn't like. It's so much better to be friends with Mark than to work with him.*[1]

Facebook now boasts a workforce of people who have all been leaders in their fields before working for Zuckerberg. As Lev Grossman reported in his *Time* article,

> *Everyone at Facebook was a star somewhere else. You don't get a lot of shy, retiring types at Facebook. These are the kinds of power nerds to whom the movies don't*

Moskovitz Leaves Facebook

In 2008, Moskovitz decided to leave Facebook. He was one of the original team of Zuckerberg's roommates, and he still holds about 6 percent of Facebook's stock. But he left the company to form his own software company called Asana, something he had been thinking about for a long time. He hopes to create productivity business software that is connected to Facebook.

In addition to wanting to start his own company, Moskovitz realized his influence over Facebook and Zuckerberg was decreasing as the company grew and became more professional. As a friend of both of them said, "There are just disagreements about the direction the company goes in, and when you've got someone who has sole authority [Zuckerberg], those disagreements are irreconcilable."[2] Zuckerberg has also shown that he is not interested in adding features to Facebook that would directly benefit businesses, which is what Moskovitz's software would do, so it was better if the two companies were separate.

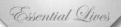

do justice: fast-talking, user-friendly, laser-focused and radiating . . . confidence.[3]

SHERYL SANDBERG

In March 2008, Zuckerberg hired a new employee who would make a big difference both at Facebook and in Zuckerberg's life. Sheryl Sandberg joined the company as chief operating officer (COO), specifically to work on advertising and generating income. Her previous job was with Google. She was especially important because of her business expertise, which balanced the fact that Zuckerberg, at that time only 23, was still learning about many aspects of business.

The incident with Facebook's Beacon utility, and the fact that it took the company too long to listen to and respond to users' complaints, revealed that Facebook needed someone with business experience. Still, it took Zuckerberg a while to decide on Sandberg. He wanted to be sure that he could get along with her because he hoped she would be part of the company for many years. Sandberg estimated that she went through 50 hours of meetings with Zuckerberg before he decided to hire her.

Zuckerberg had multiple meetings with Sandberg before deciding that she was the right person to be Facebook's COO.

Facebook and Advertising

Zuckerberg was initially resistant to selling advertising—such as the kinds of banner ads that are placed at the top of Web pages—but finally realized it was a necessity if Facebook wanted to pay its own bills. The Beacon utility had not worked and had actually set Facebook back with its users. Zuckerberg wanted to be very careful with the company's next advertising venture. As David Kirkpatrick explains,

> Whenever anyone asked about his priorities, [Zuckerberg] was unequivocal —growth and continued improvement in the customer experience were more important than monetization. Long-term financial success depended on continued growth.[4]

One of the ideas Zuckerberg settled on for Facebook advertising was known as an engagement ad. It is a message from an advertiser that appears on a user's home page, inviting him or her to do something, such as comment on a video, take a poll, or sign up for a free sample.

Spies and Facebook

Facebook invites transparency and, while many people are comfortable with this, it can have unexpected repercussions. In 2009, the United Kingdom announced that Sir John Sawers would be the next head of its spy agency, the Secret Intelligence Service (MI6). However, the *Daily Mail* newspaper discovered Sawers's wife had posted a publicly-accessible collection of family photographs on Facebook that would make it easy to determine where Sawers lived and how he spent his time, making him especially vulnerable.

The user can even click to become a fan of the product's own Facebook page. This type of advertising feels less intrusive to the user and generates millions of dollars of advertising money every year. These funds help keep Facebook running.

FACEBOOK FAME

Meanwhile, in October 2008, Zuckerberg and several Facebook employees traveled on a promotional tour of Europe. After leaving one speaking engagement in Spain, they made their way to a large van, only to find it surrounded by a crowd of fans. Several girls asked Zuckerberg to pose for photographs with them, and he agreed. As the van finally pulled away, Zuckerberg's personal assistant, Anikka Fragodt, said to him, "You're a rock star now."[5]

Zuckerberg has, despite his young age and casual style, indeed become a celebrity. But as he approached his

Facebook Advertising

Advertisers have found innovative ways to advertise on Facebook. Mazda asked its fans to help design a car for 2018 and design students from all over the world contributed ideas. Ben and Jerry's ice cream company let Facebook users tell them what their next flavor should be. In response to this kind of advertising, the companies often give away free samples—such as a free ice cream cone or cup of coffee—since they are not paying huge advertising fees to newspapers or television stations and can instead compensate their Facebook fans.

thirtieth birthday, and the site he started one night in his dorm room continued to attract more users every day, many wondered what the future would hold for Zuckerberg and Facebook. ⌐

In 2011, Zuckerberg appeared briefly on Saturday Night Live, left, with actor Eisenberg, right, who played Zuckerberg in The Social Network.

Zuckerberg's Facebook profile in 2011

Looking to the Future

When *Time* magazine named Zuckerberg its Person of the Year for 2010, there were mixed reactions. Some people agreed that he deserved the honor, especially with the way Facebook has pioneered a whole new era of social interaction on such a large scale. Others felt the honor should have gone to more important political figures. But as Caroline McCarthy of CNET put it,

> [I]t's clear that Facebook has, in fact, been at the center of electrifying change in the way that we communicate with the people around us and share information. And if Zuckerberg's relentlessly hands-on approach with Facebook—which seems to have grown even closer and more obvious over the years—is any sign, this could not have happened without the young, flip-flops-clad CEO.[1]

No matter what opinions may be about Zuckerberg personally, it is clear that Facebook is a major part of people's lives. In just one minute on Facebook, 510,404 comments are posted, 231,605 messages are sent, 82,557 statuses are updated, 79,364 wall posts are made, and 135,849 photographs are added. It is clear that

A Facebook Vocabulary

Facebook users have made the word *friend* a verb. When you friend someone on Facebook they are added to your list of friends and can see your profile. To unfriend someone is too remove them from your list of friends. Another new term coined by Facebook users is *retrosexuals,* those people renewing friendships or rekindling romantic relationships because of the ease of finding old friends on Facebook. Many people are tempted to get back in touch with old crushes through Facebook. A user created the term *Facebook vertigo* to describe how he felt when he suddenly saw the names and faces of old friends from long ago.

Facebook has become a very popular medium for communication.

What's Next?

Facebook continues to grow in accordance with Zuckerberg's feeling that Facebook needs to attract users and keep them happy before it worries about advertising and revenue. He sees Facebook as a social platform, through which other Web applications will take place. He explained,

> *It's about the idea that most applications are going to become social, and most industries are going to be rethought in a way where social design and doing things with your friends is at the core of how these things work.* [2]

He foresees Facebook as underlying every electronic device there is, including phones, GPS systems, televisions, and iTunes and providing a gateway to other kinds of applications. Facebook can now be accessed on smartphones so that users can remain logged in continually, wherever they are.

This kind of growing networking also means people who do not use Facebook will feel more pressure to join. But as Facebook continues to grow, governments worry to some degree because Facebook

Facebook users can now access the site by smartphones.
Zuckerberg hopes to expand Facebook so that it can be connected
to every electronic device and application there is.

consists of a database about citizens that is even

bigger than most government databases. It is also a

quick and easy way for people to form groups, incite

Facebook Addiction

According to a June 2010 article in the journal *European Psychiatry*, a young woman was examined at a clinic for Facebook addiction. Eight months before she went to the clinic, she had joined Facebook and already had more than 400 friends. Her parents stated that she spent an average of five hours a day checking her Facebook page on her phone and lost her job as a waitress because she continually left work to visit an Internet café and check Facebook. She had ceased many of her activities in order to stay home and on the Internet. Even during her examination at the clinic, she tried to access the Web and check Facebook.

protest, and spread information. For that reason, countries such as China, Iran, and Pakistan have blocked Facebook from their citizens. Some political analysts worry that Facebook, a company still privately owned and largely in the hands of Zuckerberg, can turn anyone off, anytime, and break connectivity to their networks and any other application that uses Facebook as a platform.

Other possible issues for Facebook include issuing Facebook credits as currency instead of conventional credit cards, which have the potential for fraud if their information is stolen. A universal payment system for everyone around the globe would be convenient but may worry banks and other money institutions.

As the number of users on Facebook approaches 1 billion in 2011, and there are currently 2 billion people using the Internet all over the world, many wonder if every single person who uses the Internet will be on Facebook soon. The popularity of Facebook gives the company unlimited opportunities to expand, but will also bring it and Zuckerberg under greater scrutiny.

RELATIONSHIPS AND TRAVEL

Zuckerberg's personal life continues to be mostly private, as he generally dislikes interviews and public appearances. As of January 2011, Zuckerberg was still dating Priscilla Chan, and they moved in together in 2010. Zuckerberg is learning to speak Mandarin Chinese, and he and Chan took a two-week trip to

Policing Facebook

Facebook is now one of the most sought after advertising mediums in history, and that means some companies do not play by Facebook's rules. In July 2009, a man named Peter Smith from Virginia saw a Facebook ad that read "Hey Peter—Hot singles are waiting for you!" Next to the ad was a picture of a woman who just happened to be Smith's wife. Cheryl Smith, as it turns out, often played games on Facebook, and she had given a game permission to access her profile data. The game company used another company for advertising, which displayed ads inside the game. But apparently the advertising company had taken Cheryl's photograph from inside the game and used it in the dating ad, something that violated Facebook's rules.

Facebook banned the company and made it clear in its advertising guidelines that this kind of data sharing was not allowed. However, as people and advertisers continue to interact through Facebook, incidents like this are likely to increase, and it is going to be more difficult for Facebook to police them.

China in December 2010 to sightsee and visit her family there. While he was in China, Zuckerberg was spotted visiting the offices of China's biggest Internet search engine, Baidu, in Beijing, fueling rumors that he might be considering a takeover of that company. He is also rumored to have visited the offices of other Chinese Internet companies, but Facebook currently denies that the company is actively pursuing connections in China.

Facebook's Legacy

At Facebook, Zuckerberg and his employees all feel they have a hand in creating something truly amazing. "It shocks me that people still think this is like a trivial thing," Facebook engineer Adam Bosworth says. "Like it's a distraction or it's a procrastination tool. . . . This is so fundamentally human, to reach out and connect with people around us."[3] Facebook project manager Sam Lessin adds, "You get at most one—if you're incredibly lucky, two—shots, maybe in your lifetime to actually truly affect the course of a major piece of evolution. Which is what I see [Facebook] as."[4]

As Zuckerberg explains it:

I often say inside the company that my goal was never to just create a company. A lot of people misinterpret that, as if I don't care about revenue or profit or any of those things. But what not being just a company means to me is not being just that—[it means] building something that makes a really big change in the world. The question I ask myself most every day is "Am I doing the most important thing I could be doing?"... Unless I feel like I'm working on the most important problem that I can help with, then I'm not going to feel good about how I'm spending my time. And that's what this company is.[5]

When people comment on the origins of Facebook, either the version they see onscreen in the movie *The Social Network* or Zuckerberg's more benign version, they are amazed that such a huge social entity could develop from a kid in his college dorm room.

Zuckerberg's Views on *The Social Network*

Zuckerberg's comment after seeing the *The Social Network* was that the movie got some things right but huge things wrong. "I found it funny," he told *Time* magazine, "what details they focused on getting right. I think I owned every single T-shirt that they had me wearing. But the biggest thing that thematically they missed is the concept that you would have to want to do something—date someone or get into some final club—in order to be motivated to do something like this. It just like completely misses the actual motivation for what we're doing, which is, we think it's an awesome thing to do."[6]

The Future of Social Networking

Despite the increasing popularity of Facebook, as well as sites such as MySpace and Twitter, experts in Internet usage feel the era of a one-size-fits-all Facebook profile may eventually be replaced by more special-ized online social profiles. Others feel the opposite trend will take place, and there will be more inte-gration of existing social networks, so that users do not have to log in to different networks for dif-ferent conversations and responses. No one is sure where online social net-working will go, but the trend is clear: more and more people of all ages are using these networks every year.

But, in many ways, it is the only way something like Facebook could have started, with someone like Zuckerberg, who in some circles would have been dismissed as a geek or computer nerd. Zuckerberg said,

> The craziest thing to me in all this is that I remember having these conversations with my friends when I was in college. We would just sort of take it as an assumption that the world would get to the state where it is now. But, we figured, we're just college kids. Why were we the people who were most qualified to do that? I mean, that's crazy! I guess what it probably turns out is, other people didn't care as much as we did.[7]

Zuckerberg's determination, in part,
has helped make Facebook successful.

TIMELINE

1984

Mark Elliot Zuckerberg is born in Dobbs Ferry, New York, on May 14.

1995

Zuckerberg begins taking lessons in computer programming with a private tutor.

2002

Zuckerberg graduates from Phillips Exeter Academy. Microsoft and AOL offer to buy his final project, Synapse.

2004

Zuckerberg quits working on Harvard Connection in January.

2004

TheFacebook.com goes live on February 4.

2004

In February, the Winklevoss brothers make a formal complaint about Zuckerberg misappropriating their idea.

2002

Zuckerberg begins attending Harvard University in the fall.

2003

Facemash is launched on November 2 and shut down that same day. Zuckerberg is later disciplined by the Harvard Administrative Board.

2003

Zuckerberg agrees to work on Harvard Connection in December.

2004

In June, Zuckerberg is offered $10 million for TheFacebook but refuses to sell. He moves to Palo Alto, California, and drops out of Harvard.

2004

The Winklevoss brothers and Narendra file a lawsuit against Zuckerberg in the fall.

2005

TheFacebook.com becomes Facebook.com.

TIMELINE

2006

Yahoo! offers
to buy Facebook
for $1 billion.

2006

In September,
Facebook launches
a new feature called
News Feed that
provokes a storm
of protest from users.

2007

In October,
Microsoft invests
$240 million
in Facebook.

2009

Mezrich's book
*The Accidental
Billionaires*
is published.

2010

The Harvard
Connection group
tries to change
the settlement,
claiming the value
of Facebook stock
was misrepresented.

2010

In September,
Zuckerberg
announces he will
contribute $100
million to create
Startup: Education.

2007

On November 6, Facebook launches an advertising feature called Beacon. After tremendous protest from users, it is withdrawn.

2008

The Harvard Connection lawsuit is settled for cash and Facebook stocks in February.

2008

Sheryl Sandberg joins Facebook as chief operating officer in March.

2010

The movie *The Social Network* opens in October.

2010

Facebook has nearly 600 million members all over the world.

2010

On December 15, *Time* magazine names Zuckerberg its Person of the Year.

Essential Facts

Date of Birth

May 14, 1984

Place of Birth

Dobbs Ferry, New York

Parents

Edward and Karen Zuckerberg

Education

Phillips Exeter Academy, Harvard University

Marriage

None

Children

None

CAREER HIGHLIGHTS

Zuckerberg created the social networking phenomenon Facebook. In 2010, Facebook had nearly 600 million users. This number is expected to reach 1 billion in 2012. *Time* magazine named Zuckerberg 2010 Person of the Year.

SOCIETAL CONTRIBUTIONS

Facebook allows people to communicate in a new way. It also creates a platform for communication with charity organizations. In 2010, Zuckerberg donated $100 million to create the project Startup: Education that helps improve schools.

CONFLICTS

In 2008, Zuckerberg faced a lawsuit by the Harvard Connection group, alleging misappropriation of ideas and deliberate sabotage of Web site launch. The suit was brought back to court in 2010. Zuckerberg also went to court against Eduardo Saverin over Facebook ownership and funds in 2004.

QUOTE

"The question I ask myself most every day is 'Am I doing the most important thing I could be doing?' Unless I feel like I'm working on the most important problem that I can help with, then I'm not going to feel good about how I'm spending my time. And that's what this company is." —*Mark Zuckerberg*

GLOSSARY

artificial intelligence
> The capacity of a computer to perform operations in a way that is similar to human learning and decision making.

elite
> The choicest or best of anything, particularly in reference to a group or class of people.

embroiled
> Thrown into conflict, disorder, or confusion; involved in.

functionality
> Capable of serving a purpose well; the ability of a product to meet the user's requirements.

investment
> Money or capital invested in a company or project to gain a profitable return.

marketing
> The act of promoting and selling, often through advertising.

misappropriate
> Put to wrong use, applied wrongfully or dishonestly.

network
> A supportive system of sharing information and services among individuals and groups.

ping
> A basic Internet program that allows a user to verify that a particular Internet address exists and can accept requests.

probation
> A trial period during which students at educational institutions can redeem failure or make up for misconduct.

prodigy
> A person, especially a child or young person, who has extraordinary talent or ability.

program
> To write code that tells a computer what to do.

project
> To calculate or predict something, especially growth or profit in a business.

repercussion
> The effect or result, often indirect or remote, of an event or action.

scheme
> A plan, design, or program of action.

search engine
> A computer program that searches databases and Internet sites for documents containing a specified keyword.

server
> The central, largest, and most powerful computer in a network, which houses the software, stores and manages the data, and provides shared services for that network.

software
> The programs used to direct the operations of a computer.

virtual
> Having the properties, appearance, or effect of something without actually being that thing. In computers, a feature or operation that simulates or represents reality.

ADDITIONAL RESOURCES

SELECTED BIBLIOGRAPHY

Grossman, Lev. "Person of the Year 2010: Mark Zuckerberg." *Time.* Time Inc., 27 Dec. 2010. Web. 4 Feb. 2011.

Harris, Mark. "Inventing Facebook." *New York.* New York Media LLC, 27 Sept. 2010. Web. 4 Feb. 2011.

Kirkpatrick, David. *The Facebook Effect: The Inside Story or the Company That is Connecting the World.* New York: Simon & Schuster, 2010. Print.

Mezrich, Ben. *The Accidental Billionaires: The Founding of Facebook.* New York: Doubleday, 2009. Print.

FURTHER READINGS

Espejo, Roman. *At Issue: Should Social Networking Sites be Banned?* Farmington Hills, MI: Greenhaven, 2008. Print.

Lusted, Marcia Amidon. *Social Networking: MySpace, Facebook, & Twitter.* Edina, MN: ABDO, 2011. Print.

Stewart, Gail B. *Mark Zuckerberg, Facebook Creator.* Farmington Hills, MI: KidHaven, 2009. Print.

Web Links

To learn more about Mark Zuckerberg, visit ABDO Publishing Company online at **www.abdopublishing.com**. Web sites about Mark Zuckerberg are featured on our Book Links page. These links are routinely monitored and updated to provide the most current information available.

Places to Visit

Computer History Museum
1401 North Shoreline Boulevard, Mountain View, CA 94043
650-810-1010
http://www.computerhistory.org
This museum offers exhibits, artifacts, and information about the development of computers and the Internet.

Harvard University
Holyoke Center Arcade, 1350 Massachusetts Avenue, Cambridge, MA 02138
617-495-1000
http://www.harvard.edu
Tours are available of the Harvard campus, where Mark Zuckerberg attended college for two years and created Facebook.

Source Notes

Chapter 1. Person of the Year

1. Richard Stengel. "Only Connect." *Time*. Time Inc., 15 Dec. 2010. Web. 4 Feb. 2011.

2. Ibid.

3. "Facebook Statistics." Facebook. *Facebook*, 2011. Web. 8 Jan. 2011.

4. Ben Mezrich. *The Accidental Billionaires*. New York: Doubleday, 2009. Print. 2.

5. Mark Harris. "Inventing Facebook." *New York Magazine*. 27 Sept. 2010. Print. 26.

6. Lev Grossman. "Person of the Year 2010: Mark Zuckerberg." *Time*. Time Inc., 27 Dec. 2010. Web. 4 Feb. 2011.

7. "Mark Zuckerberg." Facebook. *Facebook*, 2011. Web. 8 Jan. 2011.

8. Lev Grossman. "Person of the Year 2010: Mark Zuckerberg." *Time*. Time Inc., 27 Dec. 2010. Web. 4 Feb. 2011.

Chapter 2. Birth of a Computer Genius

1. Lev Grossman. "Person of the Year 2010: Mark Zuckerberg." *Time*. Time Inc., 27 Dec. 2010. Web. 4 Feb. 2011.

2. Ibid.

3. Ibid.

4. Elaine Aradillas. "Mark Zuckerberg: Boy Wonder." *People*. Time, 25 Oct. 2010. Web. 24 Jan. 2011.

5. Jose Antonio Vargas. "The Face of Facebook." *The New Yorker*. Condé Nast Digital, 20. Sept. 2010. Web. 24 Jan. 2011.

6. Ibid.

7. "Face-to-Face with Mark Zuckerberg '02," *Lion's Eye*. Phillips Exeter Academy, 24 Jan. 2007. Web. 24 Jan. 2011.

8. Lev Grossman. "Person of the Year 2010: Mark Zuckerberg." *Time*. Time Inc., 27 Dec. 2010. Web. 4 Feb. 2011.

Chapter 3. Harvard

1. "Person of the Year 2010: Mark Zuckerberg." *Time*. Time Inc., 27 Dec. 2010. Web. 4 Feb. 2011.

2. David Kirkpatrick. *The Facebook Effect: The Inside Story of the Company That Is Connecting the World*. New York: Simon & Schuster, 2010. Print. 19–20.

3. Ibid. 19.

4. Ibid. 24.

5. Ibid.

6. Ibid.

Chapter 4. The Birth of Facebook

1. David Kirkpatrick. *The Facebook Effect: The Inside Story of the Company That Is Connecting the World*. New York: Simon & Schuster, 2010. Print. 26.

2. Ibid. 28.

3. Ibid. 29.

4. Ibid. 30.

Chapter 5. Into the Real World

1. David Kirkpatrick. *The Facebook Effect: The Inside Story of the Company That Is Connecting the World*. New York: Simon & Schuster, 2010. Print. 47.

2. Jose Antonio Vargas. "The Face of Facebook." *The New Yorker*. Condé Nast Digital, 20. Sept. 2010. Web. 24 Jan. 2011.

3. Lev Grossman. "Person of the Year 2010: Mark Zuckerberg." *Time*. Time Inc., 27 Dec. 2010. Web. 4 Feb. 2011.

4. Ibid.

5. Fred Vogelstein. "How Mark Zuckerberg Turned Facebook Into the Web's Hottest Platform." *Wired*. Condé Nast Digital, 6. Sept. 2007. Web. 24 Jan. 2011.

6. Ibid.

7. Kara Swisher. "Facebook: the Entire '60 Minutes' Segment." *All Things Digital*. The Wall Street Journal, 14 Jan. 2008. Web. 4 Feb. 2011.

SOURCE NOTES CONTINUED

Chapter 6. The Harvard Connection Lawsuit
1. David Kirkpatrick. *The Facebook Effect: The Inside Story of the Company That Is Connecting the World*. New York: Simon & Schuster, 2010. Print. 80.
2. Ibid. 81.
3. Ben Mezrich. *The Accidental Billionaires.* New York: Doubleday, 2009. Print. 113.
4. David Kirkpatrick. *The Facebook Effect: The Inside Story of the Company That Is Connecting the World*. New York: Simon & Schuster, 2010. Print. 82–83.
5. "A Chat with Tyler Winklevoss," *TampaBay.com.* St. Petersburg Times, 2010. Web. 24 Jan. 2011.
6. Jose Antonio Vargas. "The Face of Facebook." *The New Yorker.* Condé Nast Digital, 20. Sept. 2010. Web. 24 Jan. 2011.
7. David Kirkpatrick. *The Facebook Effect: The Inside Story of the Company That Is Connecting the World*. New York: Simon & Schuster, 2010. Print. 83.

Chapter 7. Fact and Fiction
1. David Kirkpatrick. *The Facebook Effect: The Inside Story of the Company That Is Connecting the World*. New York: Simon & Schuster, 2010. Print. 181.
2. Ibid. 203–204
3. Ibid. 190.
4. Ibid.
5. Ibid. 202.
6. Ki Mae Heussner. "Facebook's Zuckerberg Shows Softer Side to Oprah." *ABC News*. ABC News Internet Ventures, 24 Sept. 2010. Web. 24 Jan. 2011.
7. Jose Antonio Vargas. "The Face of Facebook." *The New Yorker.* Condé Nast Digital, 20. Sept. 2010. Web. 24 Jan. 2011.
8. Ki Mae Heussner. "Facebook's Zuckerberg Shows Softer Side to Oprah." *ABC News*. ABC News Internet Ventures, 24 Sept. 2010. Web. 24 Jan. 2011.

Chapter 8. Running Facebook

1. David Kirkpatrick. *The Facebook Effect: The Inside Story of the Company That Is Connecting the World*. New York: Simon & Schuster, 2010. Print. 270.

2. Ibid. 269.

3. Lev Grossman. "Person of the Year 2010: Mark Zuckerberg." *Time*. Time Inc., 27 Dec. 2010. Web. 4 Feb. 2011.

4. David Kirkpatrick. *The Facebook Effect: The Inside Story of the Company That Is Connecting the World*. New York: Simon & Schuster, 2010. Print. 258.

5. Ibid. 274.

Chapter 9. Looking to the Future

1. Doug Gross. "Web cheers, jeers Zuckerberg's Time magazine nod." *CNN Tech*. Cable News Network, 15 Dec. 2010. Web. 24 Jan. 2011.

2. Lev Grossman. "Person of the Year 2010: Mark Zuckerberg." *Time*. Time Inc., 27 Dec. 2010. Web. 4 Feb. 2011.

3. Ibid.

4. Ibid.

5. David Kirkpatrick. *The Facebook Effect: The Inside Story of the Company That Is Connecting the World*. New York: Simon & Schuster, 2010. Print. 330.

6. Lev Grossman. "Person of the Year 2010: Mark Zuckerberg." *Time*. Time Inc., 27 Dec. 2010. Web. 4 Feb. 2011.

7. Ibid.

INDEX

ABC News, 74
Accidental Billionaires, The, 8,
   26–27, 39, 71
Alpha Epsilon Pi, 27
ambient intimacy, 67
America Online, 21, 22
Ardsley High School, 22
artificial intelligence, 22
Asana, 79
Assange, Julian, 10
Association of Harvard Black
   Women, 32
Atari BASIC, 19

Baidu, 92
Beacon, 69–71, 80, 82
Booker, Cory, 73
Bosworth, Adam, 92

Chan, Priscilla, 27, 51, 91–92
Chang, Wayne, 63
Columbia University, 40, 42
ConnectU, 60, 62
Course Match, 27–28, 36, 40

eBay, 71
Emanuel, Quinn, 62

Facebook
   advertising, 12, 49, 69, 77,
      80, 81–83, 88, 91
   blocked access in certain
      countries, 90
   going live, 39
   headquarters, 77–78
   name change, 48
   News Feed, 66–68

   privacy issues, 8, 68–71, 74
   social graph, 52–53
Facebook Effect, The, 28, 57
Facemash, 28–32, 34, 35, 36,
   37–38, 58
Forbes magazine, 8
Fragodt, Anikka, 83
Friendster, 36, 37, 48
Fuerza Latina, 32

Google, 47–48, 74, 80
Green, Joe, 32
Grossman, Lev, 24, 47, 79

hacking, 31, 77
Harvard Connection, 35–36,
   56–63
Harvard Crimson, 31, 35, 37
Harvard University, 8, 20,
   23–24, 26–32, 35, 37, 38,
   39, 42, 46, 58
Hoffman, Reid, 69
Hughes, Chris, 31, 41, 79

iTunes, 37, 88

Kirkpatrick, David, 28, 57, 82

Lessin, Sam, 92
LinkedIn, 69

McCarthy, Caroline, 87
Mezrich, Ben, 8, 26, 39, 71, 72
Microsoft, 22, 74
Moskovitz, Dustin, 28, 30, 31,
   40, 79

MySpace, 7, 9, 12, 36, 37, 50, 94

Napster, 45, 46, 51
Narendra, Divya, 35, 57, 58, 60
Newman, David, 20

Olson, Billy, 31, 32

Parker, Sean, 45–46, 50, 51
Phillips Exeter Academy, 22, 23, 78
pinging, 20–21

Reichelt, Leisa, 67

Sandberg, Sheryl, 80
Saverin, Eduardo, 38–39, 48, 63–64
Sawers, Sir John, 82
Semel, Terry, 51
Silicon Valley, 45
Six Degrees of Harry Lewis, 35
Social Network, The, 8, 26–27, 71–72, 73, 93
Smith, Cheryl, 91
Smith, Peter, 91
Stanford University, 40
Star Wars Sill-ogy, The, 18
Startup: Education, 73
Students Against Facebook News Feed, 67–68
Swisher, Kara, 53
Synapse, 22–23

TheFacebook. *See* Facebook
Time magazine, 6–7, 10, 12, 16, 24, 79, 86, 93
Twitter, 9, 94

Vargas, Jose Antonio, 21, 22, 72
Vogelstein, Fred, 51

Winfrey, Oprah, 73
Winklevoss, Cameron, 35, 57, 58, 59, 60, 61–62, 63
Winklevoss, Tyler, 35, 57, 58, 59, 60, 62, 63
Wirehog, 51

Y2K, 17–18
Yahoo!, 50–52
Yale University, 40, 42

Zuckerberg, Arielle (sister), 17
Zuckerberg, Donna (sister), 17
Zuckerberg, Edward (father), 17, 19–21, 22
Zuckerberg, Karen (mother), 17
Zuckerberg, Mark
  charity, 73
  childhood, 16–22
  color blindness, 21
  education, 19–24, 27
  lawsuits, 56–64
  personal life, 91–92
  public persona, 71–74
  Time Person of the Year, 6–7, 10, 86
Zuckerberg, Randi (sister), 17, 18, 20, 21
ZuckNet, 20–21

ABOUT THE AUTHOR

Marcia Amidon Lusted is the author of more than 50 books
for young readers, as well as hundreds of magazine articles. She
is an assistant editor for Cobblestone Publishing and a writing
instructor. She lives in New Hampshire with her family.

PHOTO CREDITS

Paul Sakuma/AP Images, cover, 3, 6, 33, 43, 49, 52, 61, 99
(bottom); Jason Malmont/AP Images, 11; PR Newswire/TIME
Magazine/AP Images, 15; Jeff Chiu/AP Images, 16; Andrew
Harrer/Bloomberg/Getty Images, 19; Philip Scalia/Alamy, 25, 96;
Columbia Pictures/Photofest, 26; Denis Jr. Tangney/iStockphoto,
29, 97 (top); Charles Krupa/AP Images, 34, 65, 97 (bottom); CJG
- Technology/Alamy, 41; Bloomberg/Getty Images, 44, 56, 66;
Eric Risberg/AP Images, 55; Marcio Jose Sanchez/AP Images, 70;
Rich Schultz/AP Images, 75, 98; Gabriel Bouys/AFP/Getty Images,
76; Laurent Gillieron/AP Images, 81, 99 (top); Dana Edelson/AP
Images, 85; Ian Dagnall/Alamy, 86; Anthony Devlin/AP Images,
89; Nati Harnik/AP Images, 95